I REMEMBER BUDDY

A Remembrance of Buddy DeFranco

3282

Other Clarinet albums that
Ron Odrich has created for MMO

Visions: The Clarinet Artistry of Ron Odrich
(2 CD Set)..MMO CD 3214
I Love You Just the Way You Are • Only Trust Your Heart • Daphne's Vision • Highway Vision • My Foolish Heart • Concerto in C minor (Adagio) • Street of Dreams • It Might as Well Be Spring • El Cajon • Two for the Road • Visions of Nina Marie • A Vision of the Hamptons

In a League of His Own: Pop Standards
played by Ron Odrich and You......................MMO CD 3215
I Concentrate on You • It Might as Well Be Spring • All or Nothing at All • If I Should Lose You • Stardust • Come Rain or Come Shine • Emily • Saturday Night (Is the Loneliest Night of the Week) • I Hadn't Anyone 'Til You • Days of Wine and Roses • The Coffee Song

Sinatra Set to Music: Kern, Weill, Gershwin,
Howard and You...MMO CD 3216
Yesterdays • Body and Soul • Fly Me to the Moon (In Other Words) • It Was a Very Good Year • Speak Low • Angel Eyes • That's All • Steppin' Out with My Baby • Prisoner of Love • Embraceable You • Here's that Rainy Day

Ron Odrich Plays Standards plus You........MMO CD 3220
Sometimes I'm Happy • I Only Have Eyes for You • Body and Soul • I Got Rhythm • What Is This Thing Called Love? • April in Paris • Porgy and Bess: The Man I Love • New Moon: Lover Come Back to Me • Oh, Lady Be Good • Poor Butterfly • Embraceable You

Brazilian Bossa Novas with Strings.............MMO CD 3276
Blue Bossa • The Girl from Ipanema • No More Blues • Triste • Black Orpheus • Meditation • Someone to Light Up My Life • Quiet Nights (Corcovado) • Once I Loved • Wave

Ron Odrich: Rondo for Clarinet...................MMO CD 3279
Rondo for Bb Clarinet and Orchestra • Rondo for Bass Clarinet and Orchestra

I REMEMBER BUDDY

A Remembrance of Buddy De Franco

CONTENTS

Yesterdays

Words and Music by
Otto Harbach and Jerome Kern

joy - ous free and flam - ing life, for sooth, was mine,

sad am I, glad am I

for to - day I'm dream - ing of yes - ter -

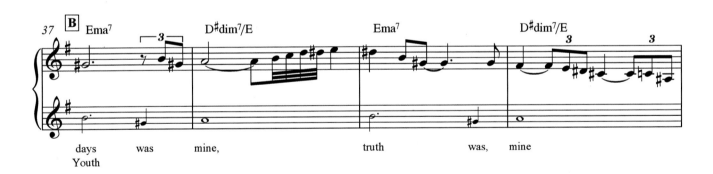

days was mine, truth was, mine
Youth

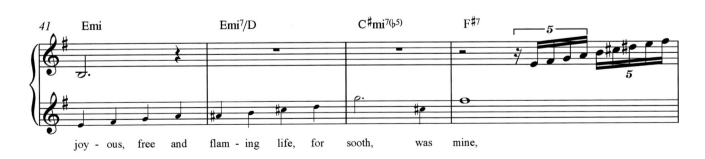

joy - ous, free and flam - ing life, for sooth, was mine,

sad   am   I,   glad   am   I,

for   to - day I'm   dream - ing   of   yes -   ter -

days.

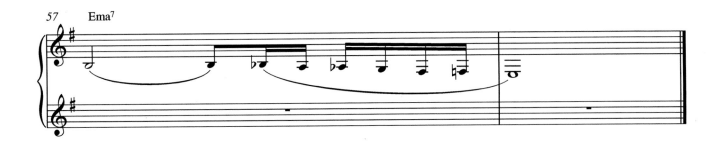

Laura

Words and Music by
Johnny Mercer and David Raksin

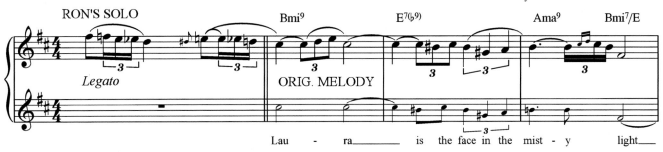

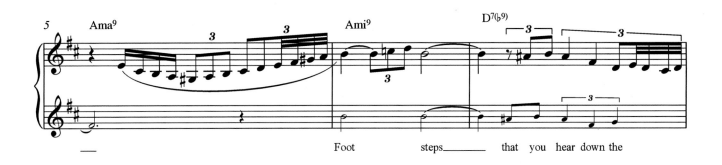

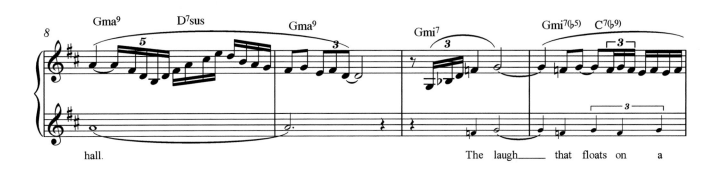

8

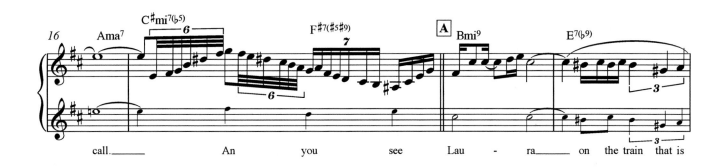

call._____ An you see Lau - ra_____ on the train that is

pass - ing thru._____ Those eyes,_____ how fa - mil - iar they

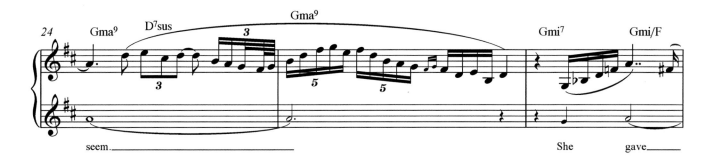

seem._____ She gave_____

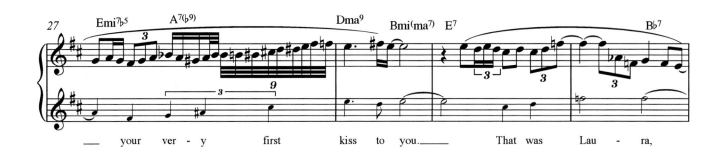

___ your ver - y first kiss to you._____ That was Lau - ra,

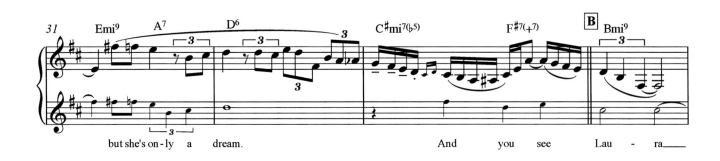

but she's on - ly a dream. And you see Lau - ra_____

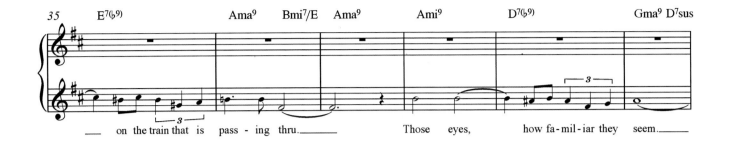

on the train that is pass-ing thru._____ Those eyes, how fa-mil-iar they seem._____

_____ She gave_____ your ver-y first kiss to you._____

_____ That was Lau - ra,_____ but she's on-ly a dream.

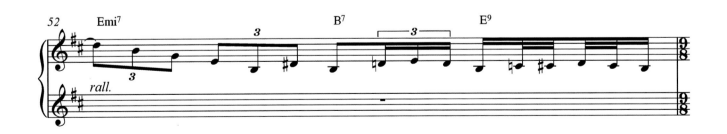

What's New?

Words and Music by
Johnny Burke and Bob Haggart

What's new? _____ How is the world treat ing you? _____

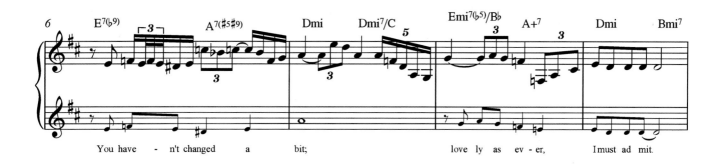

You have -n't changed a bit; love ly as ev - er, I must ad mit.

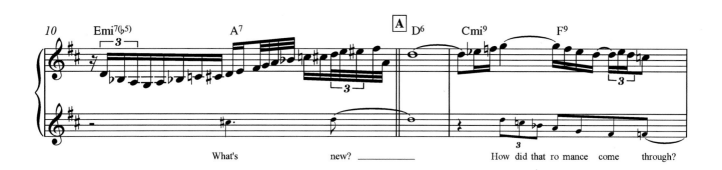

What's new? _____ How did that ro mance come through?

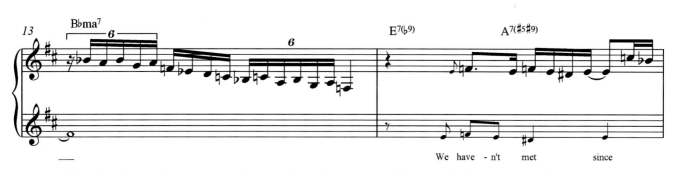

We have -n't met since

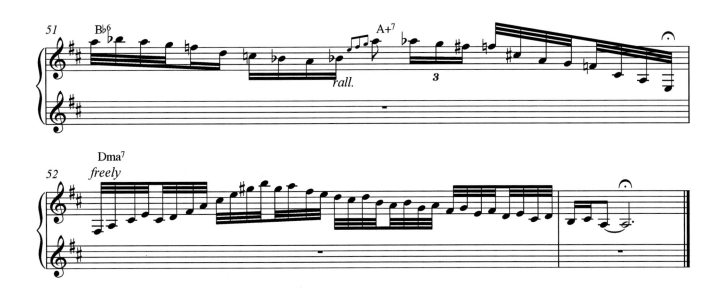

Blue Moon

Words and Music by
Lorenz Hart and Richard Rogers

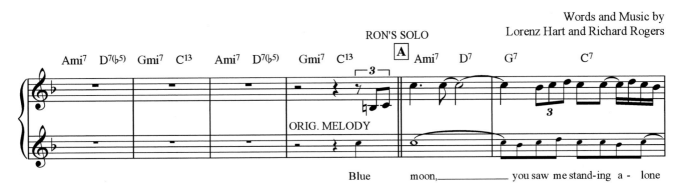

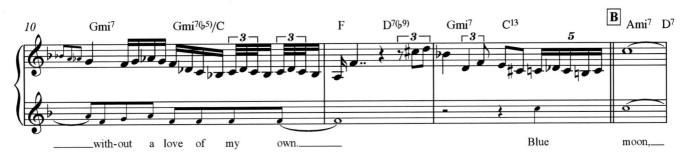

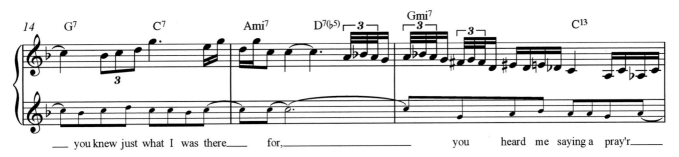

dore me"_____ And when I looked, the moon had turned to gold! Blue moon._____

___ now I'm no long - er a - lone_____ with-out a dream in my heart,

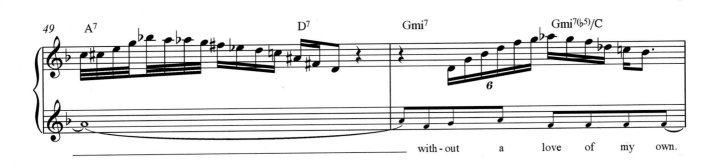

with - out a love of my own.

Can't Help Lovin' Dat Man of Mine

Words and Music by
Oscar Hammerstein II and Jerome Kern

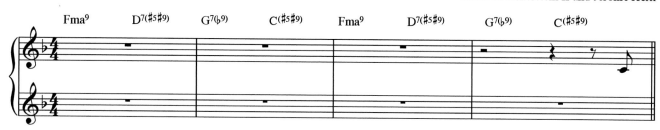

Fish got to swim and birds got to fly,— I got to love_____ one man till I die,—

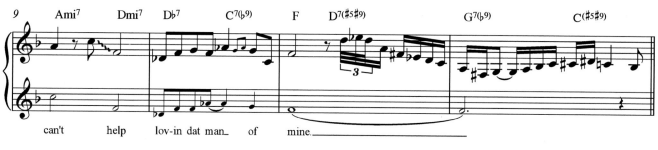

can't help lov-in dat man_ of mine._____

Tell me he's la - zy, tell me he's slow, tell me I'm cra - zy, may-be, I know,_____

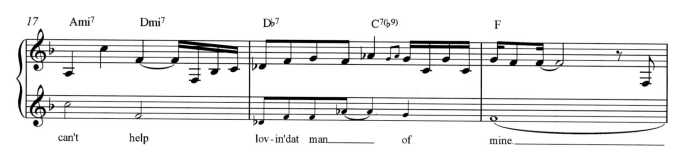

can't help lov-in'dat man_____ of mine._____

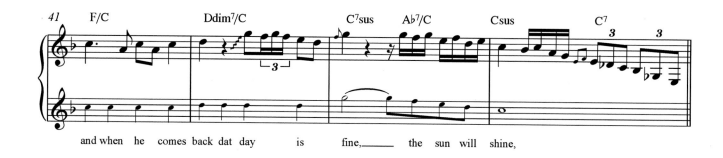

and when he comes back dat day is fine,___ the sun will shine,

He can come home as late as can be,___ home with-out him___ ain't no home to me,___

can't help lov-in' that man of mine.

freely

Embraceable You

Words and Music by
Ira Gershwin and George Gershwin

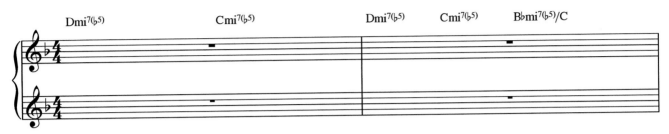

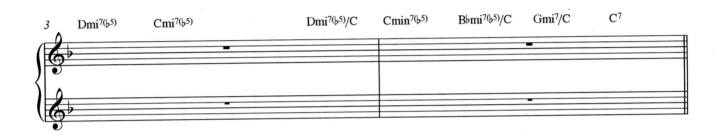

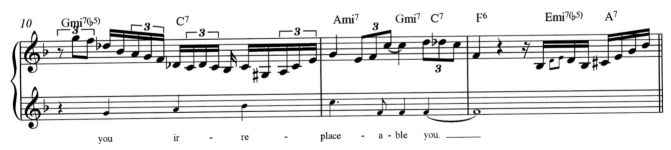

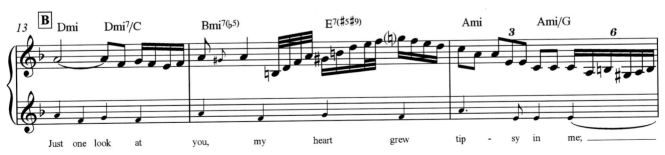

Don't be a naugh - ty ba - by, come to pa - pa, come to pa - pa, do!

My sweet em - brace - a - ble you!

Memories of You

Words and Music by
Andy Razof and Eubie Blake

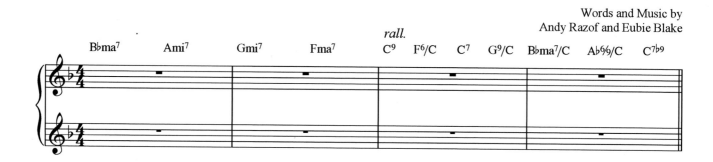

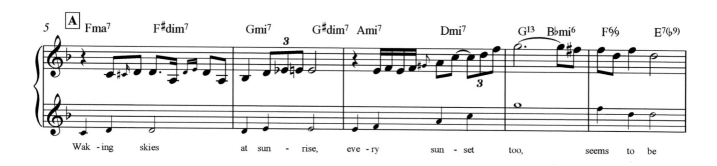

25

in my dreams   'spite   of   all   I   do,   eve - ry - thing   seems   to   bring

mem - o - - - ries   of   you.

Smoke Gets In Your Eyes

Words and Music by
Otto Harbach and Jerome Kern

hide. _____   So   I   smile   and   say,   "When   a   love - ly   flame   dies,   smoke   gets   in   your

eyes."

Stardust

Words and Music by
Mitchell Parish and Hoagy Carmichael

rubato

Some -times I won-der why I spend the lone -ly night dream-ing of a song. The

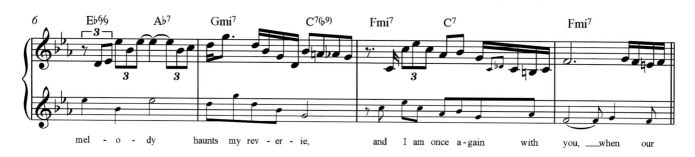

mel - o - dy haunts my rev-er-ie, and I am once a-gain with you, ___ when our

love was new, and each kiss an in-spir a tion. _____ But that was long a-go, now

my con-so - la - tion is in the star-dust of a song. ___ Be - side a gar-den

wall, when stars are bright, you are in my arms. The night - in - gale

star - dust mel - o - dy, _____ the mem - o - ry of love's re - frain.

Music Minus One
50 Executive Boulevard · Elmsford, New York 10523-1325
914-592-1188 · e-mail: info@musicminusone.com

www.musicminusone.com

MMO 3282

ISBN 978-0-9916347-9-8